Moments in Time

Moments
in Time

Love and Romance

P. Bridges-Spencer

Copyright © 2012 by P. Bridges-Spencer.

Library of Congress Control Number:	2012906570
ISBN:	Hardcover	978-1-4691-9735-7
	Softcover	978-1-4691-9734-0
	Ebook	978-1-4691-9736-4

All rights reserved. No part of this book may be reproduced or transmitted in any form or by any means, electronic or mechanical, including photocopying, recording, or by any information storage and retrieval system, without permission in writing from the copyright owner.

This is a work of fiction. Names, characters, places and incidents either are the product of the author's imagination or are used fictitiously, and any resemblance to any actual persons, living or dead, events, or locales is entirely coincidental.

This book was printed in the United States of America.

To order additional copies of this book, contact:
Xlibris Corporation
1-888-795-4274
www.Xlibris.com
Orders@Xlibris.com
114390

Contents

Acknowledgement 7
About the Author 11
My Mission Statement 15

Short Stories of Love and Romance

Moments in Time 19
Surrender 21
To Love Again 23
Missing You..25

Love Letters

Star Crossed Love..31
Letter to a Great Friend...32

You Got Mail

Club Planet.Com 35

Collection of Poetry of Love

My Strokes of Love..39
Key Master 40
Seasons and Reasons..41
The Mystery of it All..42
Friendship with Uniqueness 43
My Garden...44
You Can't Loose What You Never Had 45
Floral Fantasy 46
Passions of the Heart..47

Innocence, Bittersweet Memories 48
Eyes like Rain 49
Stillness of the Night 50
What Is a Strong Woman? 51
Song of Songs 52
Snow Flakes in the Scheme of Things 53
Defining Warm Sensation 54
Amazing Friend 55
This Man's Drug 56
Beacon of Hope 57
Things Get Better With Time (Vintage) 58
The Bouquet of Roses 59
Black Pearl 61
Drifting in the Wind 62
Another Time and Place 63
The Windows of Your Soul 64

Collection of Poetry of Love and Romance

Queen of Queens 67
Dark Dreams 68
Dared to Dream Out Loud 69
It is The Power of Love 70
Spend My Life with You 71
Two Hearts Beat As 1 72
Take Me There 73
Dark and Sweet Guy 74
The Secret Key 75
A Love to Behold 76
State of Feelings (Emotions) 77
Love in Every Room 78
Miles Between Us 79

Acknowledgement

*"Love is not determined by the one being loved
but rather by the one choosing to love."*

First and foremost to my Heavenly Father whom I am eternally grateful without HIM the Cherokee, Creek, Blackfoot Indian, African American and Caucasian would be non-existence in the family lineage of my beloved parents Willie Columbus and Daisy Williams Bridges I. Their undying love for each other produced sixteen children. I am the 15th child whom they nurtured and instilled in each child their worth and value alone with the love of God.

Each were encouraged to pursue dreams, develop their talents and work hard to become successful men and women with joy. Out of all the work put forward each took their respective places in life with some becoming successful Military Men (fighting in several wars for our country before returning home and later), Business Owners, Healthcare professionals, Designers (interior, exterior) Hair Stylists, Seamstress/Tailors, Fashion Models, Musical Artists, Creative Writers, Artists.

As the fifteenth younger child. I had the blessed opportunity to witness, learn and enjoy the growth of my older siblings. Each played a significant role in my life and found their own places within my heart, shared some of the responsibility for my growth as well.

To my sister Geraldine who took the helm after the death of our parents. A newly wed wife, young mother (first child/son now deceased) age 21, a graduate of Gillespie School of Nursing took on the responsibility and provided a safety net for her seven under age siblings age 9-18. For this I will be forever grateful to her and husband Henry L. Walker Sr. She dared me to dream out loud as well as to pursue it. She encouraged all of us to become productive men and women and carry on the family legacy.

She had put her life on hold and invested in our safe keeping something she did not have to do. She was charged to carry out our parents wishes and not allowed us to be separated. I will never forget this kind act of love.

My sister Beatrice who inspired me to work hard and think like a man in order to survive. To write what I felt and what I knew. For this is what true writers do. Made me aware that I am allergic to all shellfish/Iodine. Stayed up half the night bathing each other down in Calamine lotion and scratching each others backs after eating a spread of seafood broil during the early sixties.

To my brothers especially Walter, Frank, Frederick encouraged me to be a lady always, never allow yourself to be caught up in an abusive relationship with a man. Any man that have respect and love for his mother, sisters and other female will never break your heart to where it can not be mended.

My sisters Dorothy, Margaret, Ernestine told me there is nothing to hard for God." Keep the faith".

My older brothers Bill aka Willie II, Charles, Roy, James aka J.W. The solid rocks of strength that reminded us of our family lineage that we must stay together and celebrate with family gatherings/reunions each year.

The joy and laughter shared with my younger sibling Momma's namesake. She makes me laugh so hard to tears of joy even on today. I love each of you in a special and unique way. We will always be Willie and Daisy's love children.

To a wonderful man who gave me five beautiful loving children, one who went the extra mile when it was necessary. Thank you so much for your devotion to the family unit. May God continue to bless you is my prayer.

*   *   *

In Loving Memory of My Parents, Siblings and Grandson*. This one is for you also.

Willie C. Bridges I
Daisy W. Bridges
Geraldine B. Walker(Henry)
Beatrice B. Wright (Willie)
Ernestine B. McCoggle (Mathew I)
Dorothy B. Collins (James)
Willie II (Bill)
James (J.W.)
Roy
Frank
Robert Christopher-George Spencer

About the Author

A very shy, skinny little black girl born and raised in a South Georgia town (now Metro Status), 26 miles north of the Florida state line was given a task from day one. This was the way of encouragement to do the best you can at all times. Later on challenged to dream out loud in constant pursuit with hope of becoming a reality. Charged to become a trail blazer with energy and fierce desire in the most positive light imagineable.

Born in the year of Our Lord 1946 to pioneering Christian parents who labored with the Southern Seaboard Railroads, Woodsman Rider for a local Turpentine Business and a Shoe Repairman with Barrett's Shoe Shop. There were private family homes needed a Cook and Laundress, Farmland needed farming as well. The proud parents of sixteen children, lovingly encouraging all fourteen (two deceased as babies) to work hard at achieving their highest practical levels of goals in life. Patiently teaching them about the greatest love of all from Our Heavenly Father through Jesus Our Lord and Savior.

Heritage played a huge role in their humble beings, emphasizing 'never forget where you came from and always know where you're going'. 'To be ever so humble, gentle and kind, stride with grace, face to the sun.'

Entering the public schools at the age of six years. Learning to read, write and add along with the principles of subtraction took affect soon, being placed in accelerated classes. Throughout the academic periods of time excelling in her studies of music, reading, history, English, literature, math and social studies alone with extra curricular activities produced a graduate of her Alma Mater Pinevale High. A year long courtship, marriage took place with a young suitor who was already in the work place pursuing his dreams. He gifted her with five beautiful children. Later, with much consideration the dreams were alive again. At home, college course work began to form and take shape while being a full time Mom, Wife and Homemaker, placing readiness on the fact of becoming productive in the work place, outside the home when the time was right.

Part time factory work came into play briefly, which seems to have been 'stuck in a rut' situation. There were dreams to be fulfilled and the need to pursue them away the type work. The dream in a HealthCare Setting were part of those dreams, as the doors swung open she pounced upon it right away. The need of wanting to make a difference in the life of someone less fortunate was granted, by landing a job as a Nurse's Assistant. She continued college courses in full pursuit at VTC. She worked her way up through the ranks with recommendation from higher ups with promotions, incentive monetary raises. Recreational Services Director for sixteen years with another promotion and recommendation as Social Services Director gathering all required courses of certifications for both services under the grand father clause of law became Associate Degrees with the pursuit of a Bachelor. As the company grew so did the education process offering online classes under Pruitt University. Gladly taking advantage of to stay on top of the game and more. Serving passionately as an Advocate for her Clients insisting their rights acknowledged and respected. Aside her regular duties, services rendered to the Safety, Quality Improvement Committees as Chairperson. Wrote articles for the companies newsletter. Developed and handcrafted programs for all sorts of functions such as parties, teas. Spear headed Community Service Projects. Voted Employee of the Month by her peers on several occasions. She participated in several essay contests (judged by local newspaper columnists/writers) with first and second place wins.

A member of the G.H.C.A. of Social Workers and Therapeutic Recreational Services Directors.

Nominees for Social Worker of the Year G.H.C. A. State of Georgia six years consecutively.

Dreams and goals met throughout the years. Retirement from the work force came with humbleness and gladness with inner peace of knowing that what she was set out to do, making a difference in the lives of those she served with a passion was accomplished. She was honored by staff with a retirement party and plaque amongst the gifts. After retirement she was called back to the arena for a special recognition by the G.H.C.A. and Society of Social Workers from all Councils throughout the state of Georgia at Stone Mountain, Georgia.

A member of Thessalonians' Baptist Church, serves as Church's Clerk, and VBS Teacher for Teens. Served with the Lowndes Board of Elections as Precinct Officer. PHS Alumni Association. She was instrumental in having signed Proclamations from the Mayor of the City of Valdosta for the Bridges Family Reunion on several occasions.

Several poems published with the National Library of Poetry and Poetry Guild Anthologies in hard back volumes, Sound of Poetry Recordings, Honorary Nominees of the International Society of Poets, writings for local newspaper submitted. Featured in the local newspaper, 'Author's Poetry Published.'

Pen name J. P. Me'Velenti has significant meaning for her, each letter place emphasis on the gift God gave her through her husband. Her children names are Joaquin, Juan, Mario, Eric and Perlita. They are all productive adults with careers and families of their own. Blessed with fourteen grand children and four great-grands. An older grand son took on another family tradition by joining the Military, three are college students with part time jobs paving the way for their younger siblings.

"Inspired by the birth of my first grandson, creative writing became 'a dream out loud' once dared, my deep muse spilling over and finding its place on parchment in 1991. I strive to reflect positive images of inner peace, knowledge of the greatest love of all mankind, individuals who made an impact in my life. In hopes to reveal that romance in still alive within all of us. It should be handled with the utmost respect and care in my writings."

My Mission Statement

I am committed to painting a portrait of my inner thoughts and vision of life, love and the pursuit of happiness. In finding each without the need to apologize, with my spiritual awareness remaining intact. I am not a perfect person nor claim to be. All through my adversities I am able to maintain my faith in God.

To remember where I've been and what I may go through in maintaining positive relationships. To content myself in my surroundings so I will always know where security lies within my life. To enjoy every moment along this journey finding laughter, love and happiness with each new day that passes.

SLOGAN: Enjoy the journey not just the Destination.

Pbs*

Short Stories of Love and Romance

Moments in Time

Today is the day for the rest of our lives; we can waste it or grow in its light. Today, the Lioness fell in love for the second time around. She knows that anything is possible if only we believe. Love is never so far away or hidden. It comes when we least expect it. The Lioness is the type that does not take love for granted. She is a very seductive creature. If anything is worth the hunt, she goes at it in full throttle. She teases her prey in a subtle fashion, waiting patiently as his mood unfolds in full passion.

Her breath taking beauty and sensual moves took the Lion; he did not realize that he had fallen so deeply in love with her in such a short time. S he was having her way with him and he with her. She was thinking what her next move would be. Should she allow him to stay or just move on? Little did she know he was pondering the same thoughts? Finally without a doubt she realized what it will take to keep him around and surely she enjoyed their love making more than she wanted to admit to herself much less to anyone else.

However, as time permits and having so much responsibility of work and family. She will find a way to be with him. She knew that she was in love. She finally opened her heart (so tight, seems to have been an eternity.) The feelings seemed so unreal. Nevertheless, the plunge was inevitable. It was bound to happen at any cost. The relationship was a forbidden one and they both realized it. Their hearts overrode all the warning signs.

The Lion worshipped the ground his Queen walked on and did not mind telling her. This happened long before their first encounter. He had worshipped her from afar; she was unaware of this . . . He would tell others as he watched this enchanting beautiful hunter while in the marketplace or at a gala that she will be his and no one else should think or dream of having her. Sometimes, he would stand in the shadows admiring every morsel of her being. He had thought many times to himself that she would never have anything to do with him for he is the King of his own world and surely not hers. She had a certain style about her that even this King had doubts in winning her heart. He was use to getting his way with others, so confident that he should have his at any cost. However, he did not want to mess up any small chance he may have with her.

The Lioness wanted the Lion King to belong to her completely that she would not stop short of nothing to have him at her side forever. Little did she know he had the same desire? They both wanted the other on their own terms. As time goes by one conflict after the other kept rising in their relationship, which left each other confused and distraught for days. He refuses to give an inch, licking old wounds from past bitter relationships. He had finally met his love match, little did he realize now. Losing sight of what was real love is all bouts a long time ago.

She on the other hand, she was injured and insulted from previous relationship. The man of life she had a long history with taken on a commoner. She had neither class nor breeding. However, he had what he wished. This was heartache. So indeed the

Lioness closed the door to that part of her life. Although she did not discount the great things came from this relationship. They were beautiful tokens of love, five of them.

Once she noticed the Lion pouting about something that had happened. She moved sensually towards him, caressing his mane and cheeks whispering breathlessly in his ear sweet nothings only the two recognized . . . She said "Come my love let me fill you with my sweetness. Let me make it right for you." He became very mellow and allowed her to lead him into an oasis of love. He took her in his arms gently caressing her body, kissing her warm moist seductive lips. She not only welcomes his touch she succumbed to it. He had fed her from his plate very passionately taking the time to make certain it was just right, well seasoned and tasty. The juices from the grapes were so sweet and inviting. She is happy by the gesture she relaxed and enjoyed it.

He entered her warm moist secrets and made passionate love. Each soul was touched in a profound way. It had been awhile since the two felt so complete. To be love just for her and not out of sheer duty was simply divine. They had listened to soft music and talked into the early morning. They fell into a deep sleep from sheer ecstasy. They were both happy within each other. She had broken all the rules she had set for herself by allowing him to get close to her. She had finally let go.

The time had come for their moment in time to end; he had to return to his world without here. Sadly, neither one wanted it to end. They made a promise to each other to be together again as soon as possible. He had to return to his kingdom where he reign for so many years and she to hers. A love token left with her along with a treasure of beautiful memories with the both.**

Surrender

He craved her attention so much. He will watch her from a distance waiting for a response from her to him.

Being the careful woman she is. She will not stop short of anything to keep her dignity and self respect. She had to maintain her focus on what she felt was of own best interest. Knowing that once she let her guard down it will be all over.

She simply adored the way he had attracted her in getting her attention awhile later.

He sent messages of the affection he was having for her. He ended each with two kisses.

He wanted to feel and see her in the early mornings and at nights. It did not matter how she looked or dressed. All he knew was that he was SPRUNG by her enchanting beauty and spirit.

There was no turning back or stopping the time. He cared deeply and wanted to be with her at any cost. He shared the dreams of the two of them with her once face to face.

He'd serenaded her with love songs, courted in the market places and lounges openly.

He was well aware that her privacy meant so much to her as with him. She never really understood why he'd risk the relationship he was in already with a beautiful lady until much later.

During a heated conversation he'd blurted out "I like living on the edge ". He thought this about her also. He never thought she had no intention of hurting anyone or getting hurt. This was not her style. She knew what it's like to be in love and it's not returned and to add insult to injury the love of your life allowed another to steal their love.

Hearts do get broken as we play by the rules. It takes time to heal as well.

Time went by she decided to give the relationship a chance to rise to another level once other relationships of his was resolved/ ended. The time came for a closer encounter. The countdown began with great anticipation. They wanted every minute to count. The magic was to last for more than one night. This was to last a lifetime.

Upon their meeting each were impressed with one another. An enchanting evening of fine dining of vintage wine, the smell of freshly baked bread and backdrop of moonlight starry night overlooking a breezy ocean. Their favorite music playing in the back ground. Afterwards they slipped into a world of no retreat, no return for they had surrendered to moments in time.*

To Love Again

To love once again is seemingly a forbidden kind of love by someone who is afraid to let go their emotions be free to roam but to embrace the thought of having to allow someone to feel special feelings for them and to show those feelings in numerous ways. To love once again is to open your heart and allow that special person to come in. It is like newness and replenishing spirit.

This is what our female character Gem did. She felt as if the day may never come as she would find someone to share her life with in a very intimate way.

She had all but given up on this until finally one day. There was a notice in the local newspaper section called the obituary indicating a family member of her longtime ex-boyfriend had expired. It just so happened to be a sister-in-law.

Gems usually keep in touch with his family from time to time, checking in on his aging mother whom thought they should have married anyway from the beginning. They were sixteen and eighteen years old at the beginning of their romance.

Like any other family oriented person, she decided to extend her condolences to the bereaving family especially the husband and his mother. Gem knew what it's like to have wonderful daughters-in-law as a matter of she had two. Daughters-in-law are special people they love your sons, take great care of them, the grandchildren as well. To lose one can be a devastating loss.

She called the numbers listed in the phone book, a neighbor; an old friend of the family answered the phone stating they were out for awhile making all the plans for the funeral. Gem left a message of condolences, letting them know she had called. She felt he would not recognize her anyway since he was so small when she was dating his brother. The next step was to call his mother in a day or two.

Two days went by as a matter of fact on the day of the funeral a call was placed at the husband's number as well as the mother's. Condolences were offered and accepted.

Gem was undecided as to whether she should attend the funeral. It was a cold and rainy Sunday afternoon. She wanted to be with someone she she'd truly loved from her past. She wanted to be held and cared for passionately by this special person. She held back watching to funeral possession go past her hoping no one would recognize her as she sat watching and waiting. She had purposed in her heart that she will be with her lost sweetheart for the past before he leave and return to the coast and his life there.

Time drew near for his return to the coast. She decided to get up enough nerve to call his mother's home phone again just to chat with her and feel out the situation knowing that all her children's name will come up in the conversation.

When she reached his name she said "Allen is here, don't you want to speak to speak with him?" Gem answered in a surprised liked manner. "Oh he is here?" and said "Yes it would nice to talk with him." She said, "Well here he is" and at that point she called him to the phone. It was obvious he knew it was Gem on the other end of the phone. As he spoke into the phone with his cool, masculine deep tone voice. Her composure almost gave way. She knew there should never be anything between the two of them except friendship. Somehow she knew that a chance for them to be together had to happen.

As he spoke, he said "hello beautiful lady," when am I going to see you?" Gem was so undone she could hardly fine the words to answer him. She told him in a day or two. Assuming it was late in the evening already. She'd promised to call him the next day with some sort of plan in mind. They'd talk a little longer discussing their lives briefly. After awhile they both promised not to say goodbye anymore as their paths crossed.

Gem did not sleep well that night for the anticipation of seeing her love face to face once again brought back sweet memories. Morning came and a new day began with joy filling her heart. She was off to work singing in her heart a love song,'no more rain'. The day went well for her because she was happy once again. She was willing to love again. She able to move forward into the forbidden zone.

Missing You

Loving you is easy, making love to you is all I want to do. Catchy phrase huh? But oh so true.

How many can feel a Seasoned Woman as she speaks those words? I want to share something sweet and true to the heart with you.

Love comes when we least expect it to. We never know how, when, where it will appear. Nevertheless if its meant to be it will be. I've loved and yet I thought I had lost. I'd the urge to shut down not wanting to feel again. The pain of losing someone close was devastating to where I thought numbing the pain through others, work. The joy of it all were short termed. Trying to forget the words of my best frend "you're too busy to have dinner, movie, popcorn or a coke with me" to no avail.

It seems like it was just a few days ago when the phone rang and it was My Love on the other end saying those words. In a haste trying to explain reasons for being unavailable during the time he was visiting in the city made me feel awful. Long distance relationship can be stressful on a couples' well-being. I think back on a telephone conversation in reference to a visit he'd made to the city which I was not present. We'd spoke about all the reasons I were'nt at home made understood. Therefore, we were able to move forward and enjoy each other the rest of the evening. We talked for two hours longer than usual. We discussed different matters and through out the conversation he will pause and say I will be home at the end of June permanently." At the end of our conversation he'd said "I love you" and "I will be home to you at the end of June." I was beside myself as I listened to those words. I hardly knew what to say. What seem to have moments gone by finally I was able to whisper a few words. "Thank you, I love you too." Placing the phone in its cradle.

Time with our busy schedules as usual speaking briefly on the phone several nights each week anticipating a great life together soon. On a Sunday afternoon a mutual friend asked me 'had I spoken to him lately?' I responded with, 'not in the past few days'. It was said he had became ill suddenly and family had to rush to his bedside to take care of him. I'd kept my composure. This was unbelievable and I need to check this out myself. I thanked her and we went our seperate ways.

That evening I placed the call hoping all will be fine. The phone was answered by a very pleasant female's voice. I told the person on the other end who I was and asked to speak to him. The sound of his weak and frail voice made my heart sank. I wanted to reach out and touch the strong hands that held mine. I wanted to hold him close and comfort him, to lay his head on my lap and in my arms whisper the words he may needed to hear. I was able to tell him that I loved him, praying for him and is looking forward to being together soon. He was very receptive of this. We never said goodbye at anytime we'd spoke it was different but never goodbye.

A few days gone by I'd called again. He was too weak to talk on the phone so the message was given to his caregiver to pass alone. I decided to write a letter instead of sending a getwell card. This had to be personal a little of us put into it. During the letter writing tear drops began to flow from my eyes onto the paper. I did not understand why my mood changed, perhaps I felt he'd kept his illness to himself and did not want any sympathy from others.

The memory of dropping the letter in the mailbox on the way to church stands out in my mind for longtime. That day was Sunday June 26, 2006.

I'd had a glorious time in the Lord, worshipping and praising HIS name. His name was placed on the prayer list at church. I felt a sense of peace, calmness come over me during prayer.

After services was over and getting home. I received a phone call from our mutual friend telling me that he'd passed away earlier that morning. I was devastated somewhat, no tears, nor speaking. I was unable to move forward. Finally, I said to my friend "oh, my God we'll talk later" and put the phone in its cradle. I felt that my world stood still with out meaning. I knew I had to move forward and I did the best I could.

On Wednesdayof the same week I received a phone call with a familiar number revealed on the caller I.D. The number was my Love's number I felt happy as if I was being awakened from a dream once I heard his voice again. To my surprise it was his daughter calling to thank me for being such a special friend and my letter was well received as it was read by her and the family. She stated it was a beautiful letter and wanted to meet the person behind the words. She knew her father was loved by many back home. She wanted me to know of his demise and arrangements as well.

Goodbyes was said and hopes of meeting each other at the end of the week. On Friday evening I regain my composure and viewed the remains alone. This was to be my private moment to reflect. Saturday morning was committal rites once again I had to be brave. Our mutual friends and classmates gathered at the church the meeting and greeting was good for me. It kept me strong, from breaking down. One of our mutual friend put her arms around me and whispered to me 'you need to see him now before services start' we walk to the coffin embracing as we stood there and asked 'if I was fine'? I said 'yes' holding back the tears with a smile letting the world know I was fine. My heart breaking into bits and pieces. The family allowed our class to be recognized and sang the school alma mater and prayer. Our class ribbons were placed into the open grave also. We'd greeted the family as we were allowed before leaving the gravesite. Life must go on . . . . closure is what I thought I had as I walked away that day . . . . not !

Life is as you would have it. One can live it to its fullest with joy in the heart each new day. People come into our lives makes a significant impact on us whether it's good or bad. We simply adore the fact we have someone to share it with. When you find yourself without that significant person in your life through death or just drift away for other reasons. We may morn for a season only. We move forward eventually.

My Love came to me in Spiritual form stood at the foot of my bed with a smile as bright as the morning light. He called my name in such a delightful quiet tone. Suddenly out of a sound sleep I sat up in my bed eyes wide open and awake all I could see was this handsome man. I was unable to speak in such awe and disbelief. He'd spoke again saying "I'm all right, I'm o.k . . ." As quickly he came he went away. His presence I could feel still.

He was taken from this life what seems abruptly finally getting it right with love, life and happiness and who he wanted to spend the rest of his life with. So many words unspoken went with him. Coming back to his roots played a huge part in it as well.

His presence was felt a second time in a special song he would sang to me over and over again during our good and bad times together or when were in each others arms. It was presented to me by an unknown person at the time through cyber space with an instant message attached. The words were similar to those he would speak after he sang OUR SONG. I was mystified I felt the need to understand what it all meant was it another sign my Love was showing me? So many questions came to mind (little did I knew I had not moved forward with my life). I wanted to settle without complications. I was content with it all.

It was as if he was telling me it was fine to move on with someone new and I should live my life to its fullest with no regrets. Just as I was about to give up on my thoughts the messenger introduced himself and asked, 'where have you been?' I've been looking for you for a long time'. I could not believe this I thought. Lame line they all give a woman just to make her feel special. I wanted him to know that I was not stupid. So to play the game you would need to have a good defense without offending your opponent especially if he is a male. So the game began as he insisted on sending his phone number to call him as soon as possible. In delaying the call I told him that I had visitors needing my attention. I promised that I will call soon.

An hour went past when I made the call. He answered on the second ring. The deep smooth voice on the receiving end made my heart race. The voice sounded like my love. The conversation was short an introductory to which we are, taste in music and the option to move forward and see where it could lead. We said our good nights.

I found myself looking forward to hear from him again. I thought about it as l was getting ready for bed and as I lay there my mind went places I thought were the end when I lost my Love. I drifted off to sleep and slept well throughtout the night eventually.

As fate would have it my life began to take on another shape in welcoming someone new. I found this man to be truthful in most all his doings and sayings. Once I realized this game ended and I wanted more from the relationship. We dated as often as possible. He was a Romancer dining out at upscale restuarants on fine wine and lavishly cooked meals by well known Chefs. Roses, rose's roses and a great conversationalist and taste in music. Taking American Airlines at the spur of the moment (red eye) to places and events was no strain for him.

Wine vineyard visited with tasting and buying the ones that suited the tongue palette best.

The love making was great also. There was no settling proposal into three years of the relationship. The relationship became strained with moodiness of both. One day without verbal warning he disappeared as quietly as he appeared no questions asked.

To love and lost is good for the soul, how you deal with it counts the most. The journey is well worth the time and energy.*

Love Letters

Star Crossed Love

Good Morning,

The question was asked of me. What do I want? My answer went like this. I want to happy for the rest of my life. I want to share the joy with someone that I can love and understand their ways. One who is not afraid to share their deepest feelings with me? I want to be in love with that person of interest. I want our feelings to be mutual.

Yes my love I want it all. I want all these things with you. I want you to be with me always. I know one thing for sure. I fell in love with you a long time ago.

Should you want to hear those words? I have no problem having to say them out loud on the phone or in person.

I feel better in a sense but inadequate of not measuring up to the type of person you want and need.

The questioned is answered. I want to love for love has no other desire but to fulfill it by sharing.

Signed:

Star Crossed Love*

Letter to a Great Friend

Hello My Dear Friend,

If by chance you should receive this note. I want you to know that you are in my thoughts and prayers. I know that you are receiving the best care possible simply because YOU would not have it any other way. The Key Masters always have their way. I hope you don't mind a little humor hoping it will bring a smile and lift your spirits in some way.

I know my sense of timing isn't all that great. But I am happy that I did call you after I'd spoken to our mutual friend/classmate. You were so gracious in speaking with me although you weren't feeling your best I'm sure. Thank you and the Lady who'd answered the phone. She was very gracious as well.

My dear Friend I can only imagine what you are going through. I can only tell you what I've been through. I was diagnosed with having breast cancer in April 1998 and it was not easy. I had options and the most important decision that I had ever made in my life and that was to live my life to its' fullest allowing God to order My Steps. I refused to give in and if I had I would have missed out on some of the most beautiful experiences of Life. One experience I would never forget is revisiting my childhood, teen age years with Special Friends such as you.

Sometimes we have to redefine God's purpose for us. I can say with pride that I am truly blessed that our paths crossed again and you'd made a significant impact in My Life. Be strong and hold on to God's unchanging hand. If you need the ear, shoulder of a friend I am just a phone call away.

Your dearest friend for life wishing you much love with peace and blessings.

****

You Got Mail

Club Planet.Com

A short travel through Cyber Space takes its toll on reader who is not looking to be troll.

One may sit and Google for hours on end not expecting to be Google by a non-friend. There are so many reasons for so many searches, some out of curiosity, looking for love, family and friends. Before you know it there is a Pop up, You Got Mail or and Instant Message. In some cases it maybe a male or female reaching out into space hoping and looking whatever the case. Soon the chase is on. You be the judge as I set the scenario just for the fun of it let your imagination roam. There are two characters to this conversation not sure what gender each are. However, we will give them names, profiles you are never sure of them. Here we go hope you enjoy.

Capricorn: Hey! I was searching profiles and I found yours. You look like a fashion Model.
Virgo: Hi! Thank you!
Capricorn: How you have been?
Virgo: Who wants to know? (Aggravation noted)
Capricorn: I want to know and by the way, my name is Adam.
Virgo: Adam? A last name?
Capricorn: Why yes, it's Adam Smith.
Virgo: O.K. nice name. I am fine.
Capricorn: And I bet you are. (Flirt)
Virgo: Stop it!
Capricorn: Why? You are.
Virgo: How would know that?
Capricorn: By your profile and statement.
Virgo: Oh! Really? (With a long pause, she looked at her profile and read the statements describing who she is. Vitals: Single Female blue eyes, Auburn color hair cut short, 38-26-38 standing 5' 4". Photo showing a red tight fitting off the shoulder sweater and black shirt legs crossed.)

Capricorn: Yes! Really! I will like to meet you in person just to see for myself.
Virgo: Sounds nice, but no!
Capricorn: Why Not?
Virgo: We are total strangers. Never met before.
Capricorn: Awe . . . comes on. Let us make it happen
Virgo: When? Place?
Capricorn: Palms Park at 5th Avenue. I will be sitting near Cupid Statue feeding the Pigeons with a red Scarf. Lunch time around 12:00 noon.
Virgo: Good deal. I will be there with a red rose in my hand and by the way, my name is Eve Smith.
Capricorn: Hmnn . . . . Eve Smith, nice name and very familiar at that.
Virgo: A common name that why.
Capricorn: Yes that I know. I feel as if we had met before. (Perplexed)

Virgo had a hidden agenda herself. Do you think the photo on the profile is really who she said she is? B. Why is he feels the way he is feeling now?

Collection of Poetry of Love

My Strokes of Love

Where do I begin to tell the story of the beautiful people who came into my life and touched it in a special way. I have learned to love, laugh from the depths of my soul. Having felt caged in a world of no regrets, no returns for so long. The burst of light dared me to dream aloud.

A muse of mine is sure to define just in time my dedication to you My Dark horse, my Moses, my President alone with my number one Black Lion, my Body and Soul Mate of Deep Stimulation who knew from the start it will be Checkmate for sure. Then came the Rail Grater that said Do by You (did well by me) Now for Dark Dreams with Dark Red Wine, Seeked to find a Jay and Jay in stepping in time.

There was the Narc Boss whose drug war was sure to score undeniably. Without a doubt the Mellow Music became the theme for Man of Seduction. The Chase was on turned out to love me in a special way. You dared to look into the windows of my soul. You learned to become my Sun Shine on a cloudy day. This I dedicate to you as I dream aloud. To you my strokes of love I do provide.

Key Master

Never knew one could be so powerful
Never knew one could be so powerless
We found each other after so very long.

Secrets shared and witnessed in a few special moments.
The key to ones' heart was placed on the line with all chips down.
Vulnerability takes hold as true love began to mold

Finding you and your finding me
This is our time to be as one
Never thought this will ever be.
You're finding the key to the heart you see.

Finding you and your finding me
This is our time to be
A story that has to be told
The keys to the heart will forever be of you and me.
The Master and Mistress of the hearts bring out the joy of each.
Whatever will be because each has the key?

JP Me Velenti
(pen name)

PBridgess

Seasons and Reasons

There are reasons for each season, there are seasons when one comes into the lives of others and leave for a reason. There are seasons when we feel life changes in full bloom or just fade away. Reasons we may discover afterward or just before. We cherish each season and hold onto it dearly for all kinds of reasons.

Love is for all seasons are as a bouquet. As life, changes so does opinions and needs. Love comes into full bloom and soon withers away. Love is for all seasons. It is here to stay.
The reason for all season is in full bloom just saying hay, hello, hi to you. For the heck of it take the reins, hold on, and enjoy the ride. Life waits on no one. My goodness theses are the reasons for the seasons.

The Mystery of it All

Come with me and you will see a love so sweet one can never be a repeat. A love like mine is so refine. The mystery of it all is a well-kept secret shared once and only once.
When you close your eyes, I hope you think of me. My love will be here always this I freely give to you to have and to hold. Deep in my heart, you will have a place always.

A love of mine is a love one can never define. The mystery of it all is plain to see. The secret unfolds in action of one. See the gestures, movements, words spoken its all there.

Deep in my heart there is a light shines just for you. Come with me and you will see a love so sweet one can never repeat.

Friendship with Uniqueness

You have reached out and touched my hand as I felt the warmth of your reality. Only a step in time will lead and take us where we may need to go in poems, conversation and lyrics in song not necessary in rhymes.

The communications of instant messages, electronic mails or if we may find standard ground or air situation. We have entered a world of cyberspace. As we write, dictate or draw from a verse or two never to deny the beat of simple connection.

When in truth we shall come face to face, you will find me just as I am in hymns and rhymes. You may or may not detect shadows from behind this world we are so mechanically inclined.

We have reached out into space and found a friendship through poems, conversation and lyrics of a song, only to know the spirits of ones mind. Bursting through like the fragrance of wind song staying on the mind. My truth is my light beneath the moon and glittering stars. I will glow in what I know in verse of life and the rhyme of a new friendship. We are who we are non-perfect with faults in ownership we shall claim. We reached out, touched gently, and felt the warmth of reality.

The growth of friendship each day we found lead to sweet moments in time. Through continued verses and poems, the hearts will continue to beat simply because of finding a friendship so refined. In each, we saw and felt something that bought us in the fold of each other's lives.

My Garden

Come with me romp, play in my garden enjoys the beauty forecast.
Joyfully we find a sweetness one will dare.
Sing the song of melodious lark.
Playfully dancing to its' tune never again such a gloom.

In my garden, we shall find joy of kisses to define. The taste of sweet golden honey spun from its' maker and a small bud. Come with me let us romp and play in my little garden. The joy you will is a delight to the soul.

Kisses of life so grandiosely displayed what feelings we get to our dismay. Sing a song of melodious lark, joyfully repeatedly. We playfully dancing to its' tune, never again be so gloom. Come with me romp and play in my little garden I just made.

You Can't Loose What You Never Had

You can't loose what you never had, dreams, thoughts shift into depth of regrets.
Carefulness is a trait earned once learned. Grips thoughts to beheld were never present.
What you thought you had was never yours from the create.

The coldness faced with boldness of claiming something you never have. Filled with utterly fallacy. You can't have what you never had.
Carefulness is a trait earned once learned. Thoughts will become distinguished as time fade away. You claim something you never had.

Some things are willingly shared at ease and will display in time it's ready.
You can't have what you never had, dreams, thoughts, shift into depth of regret.
Only time will tell as it graces upon the scene. You can't have what you never had.

Floral Fantasy

Floral fantasy adorn spring's special occasion with bold romance
Midnight bloom with fluttering elegance playfully swirling about with scents of lemony passionate fresh.
Crystal shimmer in modern shapes with sexy diamonds embossed give out beautiful boost.
Floral fantasy takes delight with the hearts of the night
With all shades and scents becomes tangible to a fleet.
Imagine all the colors of a rose, lilac, daisy, tulip, lily, annuals, and honeysuckle just to name a few glistens with raindrop and a little dew.
Floral fantasy adorn spring's special occasion with bold romance give new life to a dreamer's delight.
What can be more beautiful than the backdrop of the night?
Stars' flickering throughout the night playfully keeps your gaze in sight.
Floral fantasy we give life through its beauty we do enjoy.

Passions of the Heart

Passions of the heart so warm, cuddly,
sweetness, just right with kisses and hugs oh so tight
Clings to hope, spinning so right
Passion for life does get bright just as a blissful summer night.
Sweetness as the breath of fresh, crisp, cool air
The smell of fresh fruit in its fullness bloom,
gives new meaning to words we mean.
To have the passion of the heart breaks into a melodious lark
Passions of whispers so sweetly, lightly, as a sudden breeze.
These are the things touches the heart so completely.
Passion, passion, passion sung so sweetly
of playful delights as a blissful summer night.

Innocence, Bittersweet Memories

To touch the heart and fluff and feathers of youthful days unleashes
The yearnings of yesteryears spring into simplicity days of maze.
Feelings sheltered all to long underneath the fullness of gloom.
Not even a hint of glimmer or spark of joy.

Someone touches the heart of youthful plays at a time of dismay.
The finesse of skillfulness to be savored

A lifetime of relationships now departed. So many doors without its suitable closure

The power to sustain one has come to an end of no regrets.
Time of waiting far too long the rigidness of rust sets in needing the change of oil, newness if you please
Innocence gone bittersweet memories lives on if you please

The choices one make is of their own to love and loss have truly won
With innocence gone bittersweet memories to cling
Touches the heart and fluff the feathers of youthful days
Unleashes the yearnings of yesteryears

Eyes like Rain

Eyes like rain clear and a bit disdain. Eyes like rain may never show pain.
Clear with a hint of glimmer whispers, something cannot quiet figure what it may be.
Eyes like rain clear as can be resting on a windowpane with very few things to gain.
They slip right off onto the frame.

Eyes like rain seeps of sad pain, drips right out no longer contained
Whispers of hope are sure to gain. Eyes like rain-wash away the pain
Freedom to have and to hold, healing begin to open out
The eyes like rain be clear and without pain has so much to gain.

Stillness of the Night

I love the stillness of the night nestling someplace all alone. The stars are glistening against a deep blue sea of the sky. The Moonlight aglow throughout the night. The sounds of crickets chirping away letting me know there is life still near. Beauty comes to mind at the sight, no wayward thought to enter in just the beauty that lies within. Yes, I love the stillness of the night.

In the stillness of the night, ones' thoughts are much too clearer with fondness of memories of yesteryear. What beautiful dream comes later, much, much later with deep seated pleasures? Yes I love the stillness of the night.

Oh so serene and delight once you experience a day of sheer pleasantries through your dreams of the night. Nights fall with you alone with very little sounds or none of traffic, talker, noise makers and snorers.

Yes, you welcome the stillness of the night. The thoughts and dreams of yesteryear and tomorrow you sweetly taste with such delight. I love the stillness of the night to manage a thought or two of thankfulness, anticipating newness soon to come with joy and passion in the heart.

I love the stillness of the night to catch a glimpse of heavenly light with the stars shining all so bright. You feel a slight breeze; rush of warmth next to the skin wraps you tightly in the arms of a dream. Yes, I love the stillness of the night.

What Is a Strong Woman?

A strong woman is mature, sensitive, sensual, and spiritual
She puts her best forward each day. She wakens and toils tirelessly to care for herself and those under her watch. She places her Lord and Savior above all. seeks and find to have that special intimacy.
She keeps herself free and pure until the time comes to fall in love with her spouse to be. They later become one when the time is right.

They become one, best of friends,
confidants, lovers, tending to each other's desires and needs.
A strong woman recognizes boundaries and stays within them. She is in constant prayer praising her Lord and Savior. She knows this is the pure essence of her spiritual, emotional and mental well-being.
She is a mother who practices and provides wisdom and positive examples to her sons and daughters and to the world. Her husband praises her essences to the entire world. He will never steal her love and give it to another.
For he knows she is the jewel of all jewels.
She is like a merchant ship that provides her family with the proper source of commodities. Their care is important to her.
Her eyes are of great joy, greatness, with regal gracefulness, head held high with her back against the wind.
Never to cave way to misfortune and awful deeds that comes her way.
Her lip sings sweet flavorful praises to HIS name.
She makes use of her limbs as she mends, cleans and prepares warm soulful meals for her household.
She is blessed wherever she maybe. Her light shines all around never to flicker to soon go out.
She is a blessed strong woman with all the essential credentials.
She is a blessing to the entire world.

Song of Songs

Songs of songs is the Song of Solomon's
Bride, groom and chorus
Your love is more than wine you are few with eyes
Of a dove, a delight to the heart
The voice of my beloved sings my love, my love
Rise up my fair love rise up
The winter is past the rain is over and gone
Flowers appears into the earth
The time of singing is come.
Rise up my fair love rise up
You have ravished my heart with one look in your eyes
How much better than wine is your love,
And the scent of your perfumes than all spices.
Song of Songs will forever be sung of love for all eternity
For this is the songs of songs the songs of Solomon

Snow Flakes in the Scheme of Things

Snowflakes spring out of nowhere it seems as we ask the questions, "What are snow flakes? "Where do they come from?" Most would say, 'it all depends on anyone's dreams in the schemes of things.' It may be the bloom of a flowery tree, which pops up in the spring and scheme of things.

Who is to say the frozen iced texture drizzles about in the schemes of things? Slowly in flight, it melts landing in pure delight. Snowflakes spring out in the scheme of things from zero to seventy-three degrees. There is warm delight and others cold in flight in the scheme of things. The blooms from a flowery tree, frozen iced textures beautifully displayed in the schemes of things. The seasons of spring and winter brings snowflakes in the scheme of things.

I love snowflakes and the beauty it brings, delight to the eyes and a healing to the heart. The dreamer in the schemes of things never departs. The spread of snowflakes pops up in the spring, winter and the scheme of things.

Defining Warm Sensation

Climbing the winding roads and mountains to your love anticipating what may unfold as I reach the secret treasures of your soul. There seeking and this I find scents of faraway drawing my soul within. Never to leave your gifts undefined. The tenderness of your touch is warm sensation of love to the soul.
The adrenaline burst of undeniable nectar clouds.
You are my warm sensation a creation of wonder in awe.

Waiting with anticipation as I climb the mountains to find the love which waits contained for much too long. The ripeness of the soul began to unfold with neither anticipation nor hesitation to scenes untold warm sensations of the soul.
Climbing the winding roads and mountains to your love anticipating what may unfold as I reach the treasures of your soul. Enjoying the delights of sweetness of new honey dew drops quiet so few. Truly warm sensations are well over due.

Amazing Friend

Amazing friend, endless love. I gave you me.
Completely and sweetly, forever and always
My amazing friend my endless love which that you not absorb?
Amazing friend, endless love lifts me up to heaven above.
This gift of love you receive so sweetly,
Gently, completely, forever and always
Swaying into the deep, blue sea of love
My amazing friend my endless love a love so deep for all eternity.

This Man's Drug

She transfixes your eyes on her. She is never denied of attention, never devoid of beauty.
Her movements like magical eclipses
She is a drug.
Dizziness affects you a high like none other.
Thinking of her does not bring you down it lifts you higher and higher.
She is like that white snow we call Cocaine.
The sniff of what we call Mary Jane. Calais, Viagra affecting the mind and Libido.
Yes she is you and is craved, wanted by so many of them.
The habit of you is hard to break.
The desire, wanting, with your heart rehab is required.
You need detoxification of the mind and body, salt for the wound.
Yes you are a man's drug.

Beacon of Hope

The beacon of hope seems so far away.
As you withhold what we once shared.
Between two lovers of dismay and disdain.

As the lighthouse stands against the backdrop of the sea.
That's how distant we became two ships passing in the night
Drifting about the blue sea.

The stillness of our lives seems so cold
As time goes by and new things unfold at the least a beacon of hope comes into the fold.

Things Get Better With Time (Vintage)

I just want to tell you how I am feeling inside; going about each new day with you in mind. I can hardly was it to see you again. Your love is, as the finest of wine just get better with time. I just cannot wait until the sun goes down wanting to hold you in my arms thinking of you.

I have to have to have your love to breathe freely.
Your love is like the finest of wine.
It just keeps getting better with time.
Your love has me floating on cloud nine.

I have to have your love this I must tell.
Your love is King and all is well.
Your love is, as the finest of wine just keep getting better with time
With you, I can breathe freely as our love flows evenly.

The Bouquet of Roses

A Rose is a Rose

We have so many ways of expressing our feelings through verse and rhymes and flowers.
My choice is all the above, I love the rose and its significant part it holds in our lives.
Would you call a rose by any other name? It is what it is, irreplaceable.
There are so many colors come into play, over joys one of dismay.

I love the red rose it expresses love, deep emotions.
I choose the white rose it expresses my spirituality and humility.
The yellow makes me happy, warmth and love of all creation.
Can you call a rose by any other name? A rose is a rose.

I am always grateful and appreciative with hope and grace. There is nothing more elegant than the pink rose. One that is irreplaceable. A rose is a rose. The intensities of the sun, fiery blaze, desire and pride produce the color orange.
The season of spring brings joy of so many colors.

Love at first sight with a sense of regal majesty, splendor, unachievable we have blue.
In harmony, we are at peace. The green, green rose with fertility, opulence we share.
The black is farewell to any relationship or is it just an idea? A rose is a rose.
Should you randomly mix a bouquet. It may speak of mixed feelings.

I love the bouquet of roses. The beauty the eyes look upon capturing the majestic of it all.
The rose whispers of delicacy, the need of tender care, the joy to warm a heart of coldness and despair. Outstanding is the rose when put together in a bouquet. The favorite mix of red and white says I love you intensely and with honor. A rose is a rose.

Black Pearl

I am black pearl
I am who I am
I am the best of all Gems.
I am nurtured, cultured to be the finest.
I will never be shifted by the swift currents of any Sea.
I am black pearl
I am who I am without flaw.
I will not apologize for who I am
I am love and am loved.
I have no secrets and I am a mystery.
I am your hearts' desire and yet unreachable to most.
I am black pearl and I have a truth to be told.
I am who I am
I am LOVE.
I AM Black Pearl *

Drifting in the Wind

My eyes, my heart, my feelings, my whispers to you and of you
Never reaches the point of where I want them to be.
Just like a Lion of old with courage that should never be told.
All these things just drift in the wind.

My eyes see your sensuality as my heart feels your needs.
As my soul sense your strength and whisper your name
The reality of it all and yet it drift in the wind.

My eyes shall never grow weary beholding your beauty
And yet my heart feels the intense of much pain
As I whisper your name
Just drift in the wind.

I want to tell you of these things afraid of rejection
Courage I did not have as you I had respected.
So I let these things drift in the wind.

Another Time and Place

I do not want to confuse you, its all about my love for you.
Do you really want to know what makes me fall in love?
Take me to a different time and place.

I will love you forever,
I want to be here always
Do you really want to know what make me fall in love?

Take me to different time and place
Hold me in your arms and do not let go
You do not have to say this is forever

I will show you what makes me fall in love
When you kiss me, drive me crazy
You do that for me

You ask me what makes me fall in love.
Take me to a different time and place
I will show you how and why

When you close your eyes and kiss me
You do not have to say this is forever
For only a moment will do,

I will show you what make me fall in love
Take me to a different time and place.
I will love you forever.

The Windows of Your Soul

As I look into your eyes there is a mystery, secret passions yet to unfold waiting for the right moments in time. The windows of your soul tell me of the power and passion it beholds. The world may never know for there is no rush. Your eyes reach the depth of ones soul. Revealing its' truth repeatedly.

Your eyes tell me how much you care, and yet remains a mystery.
Your eyes sings the melody of making things right, harmonizing in ecstasy making things come alive. The windows of your soul makes the secrets of one's soul explode.
The nectar of aloe, milk and honey continues to flow. The windows of your soul remain a mystery untold.

Collection of Poetry of Love and Romance

Queen of Queens

She is a Queen of Antiquity, Queen of today, so graceful and anew.
She rules and reigns as one proclaims. Her regal beauty of silky smooth, mocha color skin, coal black hair. The pride of inheritance she display so brave and dutiful.
She shall reign as well in a court we dwell.

A Queen of Antiquity, Queen of today. There is beauty of youthfulness with such grace. She speaks with voice of sternness, the flavor of honey. The wisdom she displays to the crowd she addresses. There is a song of love she posses. One with uniqueness forever to this day, a carbon copy will never do, one of a million and not a few.

She is a Queen of Antiquity, Queen of today, so graceful and few. The diamonds, rubies, pearls and emeralds she displays with a heart of gold never grows cold. The crown she wears of love and wisdom. She rules and reigns as one proclaims. She is a Queen of yesterday and of today with dignity and pride.

Dark Dreams

I love the late or early mornings. Some things about the dark dreams of the night
That leads into the early mornings, so please do not stop the continued warmth of closeness. The dampness of early evenings, the sleepiness of touching whispers, lungful sighs of daybreak never ending repeated changing of sensual postures unstill of heated fueled of newfound passions free of caged yesterdays.

I love the late /early mornings. The stars shining so bright, twinkling with all its' might sends a rush of pleasure all through the night. There is something about the dark dreams of the night that make you not want to stop of the new found passions must be free of yesterdays.

Dared to Dream Out Loud

Who am I to even think that I would dream out loud and have the audacity to stand alongside greatness of this universe? To those who dared me to dream out loud let along pursue it so that it will become a reality, and to those who paved the path to greatness for others as me. You've gave me courage to try the journey on parchment.

Maya Angelo, Terry McMillan, Toni Morrison, Charles Dickerson, Walt Whitman, Alex Haley, Robert and Elizabeth Barrett-Browning and Zane to name a few (some are still with us and some long gone). I honor and respect you. Without you a shy little girl would not have been able to dream out loud and share her dream with the world. Who's to say those thoughts written on pieces of wrinkled, faded paper which seems to be scribble, scrabble turn out to form a verse or two? At times no reasons or rhyme just prose, freedom to write a thought or three.

Romanticism, imaginary, innuendo shall never die whether we're young or old rich or poor the love of the art will go on. Self expressions of thoughts dancing in the head floods onto parchment like a steady beat of the drum. Daring to dream out loud became a challenge filled my soul. I must succeed I tell myself, give it some light, the scribble, scrabble was born.

To those I named above and those I have not. I applaud your greatness in a special way. My unsung Heroes My family, classmates of my school days, the first grade into Pinevale High. The roots that kept me grounded to this day.

I call it love and this is what it's all about. You kept me in your hearts because you love me. I will always love you and just to think I have the audacity to dream out loud.

It is The Power of Love

We have love, peace and happiness
We got the power; we got the power of love
Can you feel the power, can you feel the love
We got the power of love.

It is the greatest love of all
We have to tell the world about this love
When we walk hand in hand underneath the blue skies
We got love; we got the power of love.

We stand to show the world we got love
Kisses in the breeze on a summer eve is all we need
We got love, sweet good love
When we walk hand in hand with our feet in the sand

We got love, sweet, sweet love
We got the power of love
When our hearts beat as one, we got love
We can tell the world about this great love
It is the power of love.

Spend My Life with You

Please give me one night with you, everyday for all time.
Just one night with you, one day, one hour
Everyday of our lives, it will be so nice
Give me one night, one day, one hour for life.

Everyday of a lifetime it will be so nice.
I am hoping and praying you want this too.
One night, one day, one hour
Just call my name and I will come running

I will give you my all everyday we are together
One night, one day, one hour
I will be there right by your side
I want to spend my whole life with you,

It feels so good when you near me.
Just say the words and I will come running to you.
One night, one day, one hour
Everyday of our lives, it will be so nice

Two Hearts Beat As 1

I can feel your heartbeat as it races with time. Your heart and mine beats as one.
Your body gives off energy of warmth and divine when it is next to mine.
Touching with great anticipation, what wonders of creation?
There is so much static sensation opens the doors to your love of fixation.

Your enery draws me into its love calling out my name, speechless I am.
Two hearts beats as one as the senses swell
Our love unfolds with appreciation one moment at a time.
I can feel your heartbeat as it races with mine.

We touch with great anticipation when the feeling is right.
Never to be ashamed, no one to blame, this flame have a name.
Our love unfolds with appreciation of this creation.
Two hearts beats as one with much appreciation.

Take Me There

Take me there in songs and poems, never mind the rhymes
Take me there I want to hear the sounds
I love the smoothest jazz of jazz

Just take me there, let me feel the vibes
Make it smooth as smooth can be, take me there
To a real quick love of some, smooth jazz

I want to feel the vibes of a real good groove
Take me there with your smooth moves
The jazz with class got me in the mood.

Take me there in songs and poems
A love like mine is hard to define
There is no need to kick a rhyme

Let me feel the vibes, make me float
Take me there on a musical note
I love the smoothest jazz of jazz this you know.

To a real quick love affair of some smooth, smooth jazz
This I must have just like the finest of wine
Take me there in songs and poems.

Dark and Sweet Guy

Darkness with this sweet person can be any woman's blessing.
The flavor of any woman's desire
His heart is like the white snow
He seems so pure and simple, cool calm and collective.

A gift from heaven above and yet a mystery within itself
A woman may never know the reason why her senses come afloat'.
This dark and sweet person comes about, what a delight.
A flavor of one's desire remains a mystery from on high

Darkness with this sweet person is such a mystery.
The feelings you get make one shiver, yet so nice
A woman's pleasure and delight
See how the two soon take flight.

The Secret Key

The motion, rhythm, harmonizing, drifts into deep passions of sweet desire.
Never before felt so complete going through motionlessness, had rhythm, feeling so unfulfilled. You came into my life went places no one has before, dared to reach my soul.
You demanded to take control, of my secret key.

The motions, rhythm floating on a sea of passion until the nectar of my soul flowed.
Together we reached the heights of sweet ecstasy.
The nectar of love intertwined into beautiful flavors of melody.
Harmonizing the secrets of our souls of ohm and ah.

Together makes it alright, daring to reach the souls, never to grow cold
Playing with feelings of a grand piano
Harmonizing the secrets of the soul to be told as the key is now unfolded.
The secret key to my soul is now bestow.

A Love to Behold

Love between two lives on forever as he shower her with sacred gifts
He adorns her with sweet kisses. He speaks the words she is thinking.
She was speechless with the greatness of joy. Her mind swirls with words "Dear Sweet Jesus, Is this real?" Her thoughts were then answer; with sweetest smile, he took her hands.

Gazing into her eyes oh so kindly, gently touching her lips and said, yes, this is real."
You are for you and me for you . . . We are free to have and to hold from this day forward as we grow old. She sweetly concedes anticipating what a love to behold.

State of Feelings (Emotions)

I am watching you as you watch me. I am feeling your presence in every way. I sensed the same from you, you are feeling me and I am feeling you there is great pleasure knowing this. What scenery each holds as we looked into the windows of each soul. I love each moment of your nearness while holding you so tenderly.

I never thought this would ever be our souls saying yes of you and me. I am watching you as you watch me feeling each presence in every way. Our emotions romp and play so freely, so happy just you and me. This should be forever just you and me.

Love in Every Room

Loving all of you in every place, we share, when we placed our hearts and love in every room. The nectar, touch and scent all so sweet. Loving all of you in every room gives delight and pleasure in every way. You touch my hand, heart and lead the way into a world of pure ecstasy.

You came into my life like a rushed wind; there you stayed for a moment in time. Loving you in every way brightens each new day in a very special and unforgettable way. Love in every room gave new meaning that life is what we want it to be. We love each other in a special way with no bars to hold only just you and me. Freedom to love in every room we see.

Miles Between Us

You and I are far away distances between us. Oh, how we anticipate nearness not far away. You exist in every breath I take. I can feel you with every beat of my heart. There is no other love like ours. I am with you and you are with me during the good and bad times. W are together in love, spirit no matter what the physical distances.

You can into my life and stole my heart like a thief in the night. The miles between us will be few, as we became one, bone of my bone. You are my all in all, there to catch me should I fall. Just as the lyrics of our song, miles between us will be none.

Made in the USA
Columbia, SC
21 February 2022